Happy H
Marie Alessi

Influencer ♥ Speaker ♥ Author
www.MarieAlessi.com

Copyright© 2022 Marie Alessi. All rights reserved.

The people and events described and depicted in this book are my very personal story, how I perceived and experienced it. If advice concerning any professional matters is needed, such as legal advice or psychological, the services of a qualified professional should be sought. This book is not intended for use as a source of psychological or medical advice.

There are no guarantees my approach will work for you; the tools, stories and information are provided as examples; they worked for me, my family and a lot of my clients – some of them will be named in this book. Every journey is as unique as the person experiencing it.

First Edition February 2022 | Copyright 2022 by Marie Alessi

All rights reserved. No part of this book may be reproduced, stored in a retrieval system or transmitted in any form by an electronic, mechanical, photocopying, recording means or otherwise without prior written permission of the publisher, Marie Alessi.

Photo Credit: Stine Jensen Photo©
Editing: **Sharon Baillie**

You can join my movement here:
https://www.facebook.com/groups/LovingLifeAfterLoss

Table of Contents:

♥ Introduction

♥ **H**appy ever after

♥ **E**mily, Epiphany & Empowerment

♥ **A**round the world in 60 days

♥ **L**ove is all there is

♥ **I**ntuition is your Guide

♥ **N**urturing Healing Habits

♥ **G**ratitude is your SuperPower

♥ About the Author

♥ Free Gifts

♥ Thankyous

Introduction

I believe we all have at least one book within us. I have wanted to write an Autobiography since I was about 12. In fact, I found the first couple of pages of it when I was in "extreme decluttering mode", about 2.5 years after my husband's passing. It made me smile. The dreams I had about my life included romance, a knight in shining armor, 2 kids & a "happy ever after". None of them included a dead husband, yet everything else came true...

When I found myself labelled as a *widow* at the age of 45, I rapidly grasped the crossroad life had presented me with – and it was a perfect reflection of what Rob had taught me years prior to this very moment. I heard it echo in my head in his voice: "You have 2 choices babe!" I knew what I would choose, just like I knew what I chose with Rob: **Happiness!**

When I wrote my first book "Loving Life after Loss" I decided to share our story with the world. How we met, fell in Love, created our dream life – the barefoot wedding at the beach, a house, 2 kids... and then how Rob passed and the first couple of months of how we dealt with it. Little did I know that our story not only became an Amazon No. 1 Bestseller, it also ranked in the top 100 of Australia... that's when I knew I had something the world needed: **Hope!**

This is my 2nd book. **"Happy Healing"** ...because that's exactly what I chose over and over again, at every single crossroad presented to me in my "life after Rob". My biggest inspiration for that choice are our two beautiful boyzz, Flyn and Jed, and a promise Rob and I had given each other; you know, those moments when you hear about tragic, fatal accidents on the radio... "If something was to ever happen to me, I'd want you to create the happiest life possible for you & our boyzz" – we both meant it from the bottom of our hearts. That's what Love is all about: you want the other person to be *happy*.

Every ending is a new beginning, an opportunity, a blank canvas – yet accepting this doesn't always come easy, in particular when it means saying goodbye to the Love of your life, father of your two boyzz.

And this is where I will start my second book!

Allow me to take you on a **Healing Journey...**

♥ ♥ ♥

To **Rob**, for your unconditional Love, lightness & laughter.
For always making me feel like the chosen one,
and for the incredible gifts that keep on coming!

To **Jed**, for your soft heart,
kindness, patience,
cheekiness & empathy.

To **Flyn**, for your calmness,
wisdom,& strength well
beyond your years.

You are the true SuperHeroes in my life and
your hugs are so comforting for me!

**Thank you,
I LOVE you!
xoxo**

Happy ever after

Rob was my knight in shining armor; an absolute gentleman, lover for life. Food was his passion, the ocean his second home. We lived the dream that every girl dreams about...
I remember the first time I saw him; he was oozing happiness & lightness. Everything with Rob was easy. I didn't even realise when I fell in Love with him. Contrary to my relationships before Rob, with lots of fireworks & an equal amount of ashes later, this one started with a little flame that was burning brighter each day - and grew into that fire between us...
And once I knew, there was no more hesitation.

Our story is told in a heartbeat. We met in May, Rob moved in with me in August, proposed in October, under the stars on a Houseboat, anchored on the Hawkesbury River - and we celebrated our barefoot wedding in March. Something we both had been secretly dreaming about our entire lives.

I always thought we'd be one of those couples you see on retirement catalogues, both wearing white linen, holding hands, walking the beach... Just like we did on our wedding day.

Yet we had a different soul contract. I have no words how much Love it takes to "sign up" for a contract like that. Rob impersonated that amount of Love.
And dare I say the Love I experienced in those 13 years I was gifted with this incredible man, others often only dream of.

I was Rob's Queen. He put me on a pedestal at every chance presented to him. I was his chosen one - a feeling I had been longing for my entire life. It was the "Happy ever after"
I always believed in.

And then life changed in an instant. Rob went on a business trip and never returned home.

We had our last conversation over the phone on Monday night. He was tired; it had been a long day for him. We talked about Love and how he met a young couple that invited him to join them for dinner at the restaurant where he ate that night. "I think I left them with a lot to think about" Rob said. After our "I love you" we hung up.

The next day Rob was meant to wake me. Yet the clock ticked over to 7.31 without a phone call. Very unusual for Rob - he was always on time. My anxiety levels rose after every unanswered text and call. I kept trying to ring him all morning… And then in the afternoon the phone rang. I saw the number, indicating a land line from Western Australia, and knew it was about Rob.

A sergeant from the *coroner's office*. Here's a bilingual moment for you: this was my very moment of learning the word "coroner" hands on. His words still echo in my head: "I am sorry to inform you that your husband deceased in a hotel room in Perth this morning."

My world stood still.

Emily, Epiphany & Empowerment

The first couple of weeks after Rob's passing were a blur. I went into "functioning mode". The boyzz became my main focus.
I watched them like a hawk, made sure I was always on standby, holding space for them, holding them yet still giving them their space to just be.
I was constantly gauging their mood.

When I think back of that time now, over 3 years later, it feels like watching a movie back in timelapse - everything around us moved so quickly, only that I felt like the one in observer mode, hardly moving at all. Yet there was so much to organise, so much paperwork, the funeral, the uncountable phone calls…

And my nervous breakdown.

That I remember quite vividly. Approximately a week after the funeral I collapsed.
It escalated so quickly I couldn't stop myself - and again, I remember it from the observer position, almost like an "out of body" experience. The boys were having an argument over brushing their teeth, I asked them to stop, they didn't – and I heard myself yell out "I just need peace and quiet!".

It was such a key sentence for me.
As soon as I said it out loud, I shouted it; again and again.
"I just need peace and quiet!"

And with every single time this sentence came out of my mouth, it came with more force.
It was like a valve had opened up that could not cope with the vehemence of the emotion behind it. I screamed "I just need peace and quiet!!"

Then I fell to pieces, screaming on top of my lungs, just screaming; and whacking kitchen cupboards that till this day wear the chips to carry that memory of my collapse.

I felt so empty. Sitting on the kitchen floor, watching myself after the breakdown. I was wondering whether my neighbours were calling someone right now. I even contemplated whether it would be the police or an ambulance collecting me off the floor. But nothing happened. The silence was deafening.

Then it felt like a bolt of lightning piercing through my heart... The boys!! The house was so quiet. My mum had disappeared into Jed's room downstairs, the boys were still upstairs. *Open plan* means there are no doors to hide behind. They received the full vehemence of my meltdown. It broke me. I knew there was *nothing* I could do or say to take this back.

I walked upstairs and found them both in my bed. Flyn sitting there, speechless, and Jed hiding under the doona. My heart sank seeing them like that. I had no words. I felt I had caused a damage that I could never repair. In that moment I knew I needed to get help.

It was a pivotal moment; I dare say the start of my healing journey – and also the seed planted for something way bigger than us.

Yet first I had to deal with my boys. I felt so broken, knowing fair well I had not enough strength left that could've prevented the damage I had just done. I had no idea yet how important this very moment was for all 3 of us.

Jed sat up with a blank look on his face. "Were you scared?" I asked. He nodded. "So was I!" I truthfully agreed. I was lost for words. Seeing them, I just wanted to cry. I felt so guilty for not having had anything left to protect them – protect them from my own outburst.

"You know how you've got Doreen at school?" I continued... Doreen was the lovely school counsellor who saw them both at least once a week - or whenever they needed a break. "Yes?" Flyn looked at me in anticipation. "I think I need to see somebody too!" I added.
"I think that's a good idea." Flyn responded, wise beyond his years.

I hugged them. I apologised. I wanted to make it all disappear, undone. Never happened. The pain of seeing them so scared infused me. Yet it was part of our story.

The next day I rang Emily. Emily was the most beautiful person; calm, wise, kind. I had her on my list of emergency contacts for clients. In my coaching business I would come across people that I was not equipped to deal with. Suicide was one of the topics I would not touch. Twice in my coaching practice I was approached with this topic and I listened, held space and referred them on. I am a coach, not a counsellor. Emily was a positive psychologist. I had never spoken to her in person before, but in my heart I already knew that she was the one I wanted to speak to. She came with high recommendations from a fellow coach.

Although she wasn't taking on any new clients at that stage, when she heard about me, she rang me back - and after our short conversation, she offered me one of her emergency spots. I instantly felt relief. Only 3 days later I sat in her office.

My journey with Emily was short yet powerful.

Coaches are either the easiest or the most challenging clients to work with. You can come across coaches who sit in their "I know it all" bubble, dissecting every word you say to squeeze it into their own scheme. I have been there once before. It's not a great space to be in, as "I know" is the end of learning. It's also a conversation stopper, closes all doors.

And then there are coaches who meet you with curiosity and an insatiable thirst for learning. This was the state I was in when I met Emily. Each session with her opened my heart and mind further to the opportunities of healing.

One day I found myself sitting with her and gazing at the most beautiful view from her office. "I find it so exhausting, how people *expect* me to grieve and fall apart" I shared with her. And she looked at me with her beautiful face, no judgement, just kindness – and asked me ever so calmly "What does grief mean to you, Marie?"

This very question was the beginning of it all. In Emily's office, with her simple question that got straight to the point, I had the most enlightening epiphany.
"Empowerment!" I answered, to my own surprise.

Wow.
I did not expect that.

And yet, it felt so true. I had never felt so empowered through any other experience in my life, other than my two births (yet they would fall under the chapter "Happy Birthing", not to be found in this very book).

And there it was. A word that shifted my entire perspective on grief. One word that inspired me to write my first book.

"Loving Life after Loss" was published in October 2018. The day after publishing day it had not only become an Amazon no.1 Bestseller, but it also ranked in the top 100 of Australia!

This really blew my mind. I remember seeing my book with the no. 61 next to it – and then Michelle Obama's "Becoming" at no. 16 – it literally felt like rubbing shoulders with the former First Lady, being featured on the same list with her...
Talking about feeling empowered!

Needless to say, I had to buy *Becoming*. I loved every minute of it.

Around the world in 60 days

Rob & I had planned to take the boyzz travelling around the world for an entire year. We wanted to take 2019 off, home-school the kids and enjoy an adventure of a lifetime. Well, it seems like not only our plans were drastically changed, but the entire world was restricted in their travel plans.

When Rob passed, our funds were frozen. I was literally without cashflow for 19 months! That's how long it took for his final death certificate to come through. I often wonder how some families survive - not only dealing with the emotional waves, but not having access to any of your finances whatsoever.

I wasn't only lucky enough to have an amazing accountant and lawyer, but also very close friends who put a GoFundMe page together for us. We have been blessed and looked after in ways I cannot describe with words. Yet *one* friend (who wants to remain anonymous) showered us with generosity & said "do something that makes your heart sing!" And so I did.

I decided to do a mini-version of what Rob & I had planned to do together. I still have the entire itinerary of our trip in pictures stuck on our wardrobe at home. We wanted to start through South America, which to date patiently awaits its turn on my bucket list, then continue through Europe, finally show my m3n Vienna in summer, come back through Asia and then home... We literally planned an entire year of summer.

I knew I wouldn't feel safe enough to travel through South America on my own with our two boyzz at the ages of 10 & 8. I also did not feel in the right state to be home-schooling *two* kids on my own. And I knew I wanted to *not* be home for all these first anniversaries coming up; Christmas, New Years and both the boyzz' birthdays. I wanted to create new and happy memories for them, for us; honour what Rob & I had always promised to each other... "If something was to ever happen to you, I want you to create the happiest life possible for you & the boyzz."

Of course, when we talked about it, it felt like theory. Now that it has become our reality, who was I to not honour this promise? I needed it. *We* needed it. So off to the travel agency I went. A couple of destinations I already had in mind that needed to fill our itinerary - yet we had lots of room to play with, thanks to the generosity of my beautiful friend. The money we received not only paid for the entire trip, it also lasted for the rest of the year and much more.

It took me 3 trips to the travel agency before I had the courage to hand over my credit card and make the booking. I remember sitting in the car when this song came on the radio "I want you to have it all" by Jason Mraz. I had never heard that song before, even though Jason Mraz was on our list of favourite artists. It melted my heart; I knew it was a sign from Rob. The day I finally booked and jumped back in the car, the exact same song came on!

Allow me to take you on a shortcut of our trip around the world... ready? Buckle up!

One of the first stops I had in my heart was **La Palma in the Canary Islands**. My godfather Ricardo had migrated to this beautiful place around the same time when I moved to Australia. I never had the chance to visit him there - and this time I knew I had to be there.

Yet Ricardo had a very particular time window for us, to give us his full attention; so, we had 1 week to spend before we would get there. I remember standing in front of the big world map in the travel agency, musing about where between Sydney and La Palma we could spend one week. It literally jumped out at me and I exclaimed with a massive smile on my face "**Maldives**!".

I once travelled to the Maldives with a boyfriend at the time - and I always wanted to come back and stay in one of those amazing overwater bungalows. So, my trip was complete. I kept the first and the last stop a secret, everything else I shared with the boyzz.

The hardest part of keeping it a secret was that we had to spend one night in Malé, the capital, before the boat would take us to our island the next day.

Funny side story: 2 of our 3 suitcases didn't arrive with us. We only had the one with all our winter gear! Hilarious... not!

When we finally sat in that boat, I was enjoying watching my boyzz looking at the islands that we passed... still no clue where we were going. When we boat stopped and we got off at our island, the look on their faces was priceless. A lady showed us around on a golf buggy and when we slowly rolled across the path to our overwater bungalows, my surprise was complete.
Of course our hut was no. 12!
I shared in my first book how I kept seeing the numbers 12, 6 and 126. Rob passed on June 12. I always knew he was near when I saw those numbers - and we saw them *a lot* on our trip. It made my heart sing.

All 3 of us were blown away by the beauty of this island. Well needed rest, softness and nothing to do but just *be*! My soul soaked up this break, just like my body soaked up the sun. I could feel a weight slipping off us, being carefully replaced by lightness and ease. It was absolute bliss. I felt like my soul was finally catching up with my mind, reuniting, high-fiving each other for what they had mastered over the past 5 and a half months. It felt so surreal, so far away and yet it had become part of us, who we are.

I also shed a few tears in paradise... We kept sitting at the same tables, set for 3. And one night Flyn chose a different table. It was closer to the buffet, which made me smile, as both the boyzz had made friends with one of the chefs there. He was always happy to see them and treated them like VIPs. After the boyzz went off to pick out their favourite choices, a waiter came and took the 4th set away. When he left, I burst into tears.

The simple act of collecting the plate, glasses and cutlery broke me, as it symbolised and highlighted Rob's absence. I eventually shared with the lovely young waiter who we had grown so fond of, what happened. To see the look on his face showed me how deeply touched he was...

After a week of serendipity dipped in serenity, we departed from the island that had won our hearts. The staff had been incredible - you could tell how much they had allowed us into their hearts. Photos were taken, hugs were shared - they don't host kids very often and had really taken to Flyn & Jed.

Landing on **La Palma** was such a stark contrast to the white soft island. Volcanic formations, black beaches, harsh, yet incredibly beautiful in its own way; I almost melted into my embrace with Ricardo who awaited us at the airport.
He was a very important influence in my life - in particular after my dad passed when I was 20.

I needed his peaceful presence so much and was grateful that he offered us one of his guest houses to stay with him!

Those 9 days were filled with so much Love, the most honest talks anybody had with me since Rob's passing, real heart-to-hearts. I was longing for what Ricardo offered so freely... Back to nature, playing ping pong & drinking lemon grass tea, long walks & talks to feed my soul.

Ricardo had the ability to ask questions so directly and without offence, that it opened my heart to possibilities of healing without even noticing how much society was blocking such endeavours.

When we left La Palma, I felt so enriched. I had never spent so much quality time with Ricardo before. Our next stop was **Austria**, with a whole lot of family and friends waiting for us. I wasn't too sure how I felt about going back to my roots... It felt a little overwhelming, in particular with Christmas approaching with huge steps - our first Christmas without Rob.
The next couple of weeks I experienced a lot of different emotions. It was deeply nurturing to be with people who knew me so intimately - yet on the other hand I felt how much I had changed since my last visit. Widowhood changes you. Being a sole-parent changes you.

You know that feeling when you haven't seen your family in forever, and as soon as you reconnect, you seem to be falling into old habits and patterns, no matter how much you have changed? Not this time. For the first time I felt *allowed to be different*; almost as if I had needed a good enough reason to be granted permission to change. Bizarre, isn't it?!

Christmas was pretty much non-spectacular, in a very peaceful way. We bought a little real life tree - something that is rather rare in Australia and very common in Austria. I watched the boys hang decorations, a tradition that was always filled with so much joy in our home. Rob and I used to help less and less over the years, as Flyn and Jed had grown old enough to decorate the tree themselves - and they took so much pride in it. It always filled my heart with joy watching them. Now it felt bittersweet.

I thought I might fall apart. I didn't. We went to the movies and watched the Grinch in 3D. It sprinkled a little magic over our Christmas, watching the snow fall in the entire cinema, as if we could touch it... To be honest I was glad when Christmas was over. No, I didn't turn into the Grinch myself. Yet the anticipation - worrying about how our boyzz would cope, spending their first Christmas without dad - had weighed heavily on my heart.

My mum had moved into my apartment when I moved to Australia; so, whenever I'm back in **Vienna**, it feels so beautifully familiar - even though the place is so different now that my mum lives in it. One afternoon I was sitting on my bed allowing the wave of "moments since Rob's passing" to wash over me. I thought of the incredible honour of  finding out that my first book "Loving Life after Loss" had become an Amazon no.1 Bestseller *and* ranked in the top 100 of Australia. I set off on a short trip down memory lane...

And there, in my birthplace Vienna, something else was born. I realised that our story was so much more than just a book; I could feel this deep urge rising within me to do something bigger with it. And what I put out into the universe came back in the form of an email from my future mentor, who specialised in building movements. That's exactly what I needed to do - creating a movement for people needing hope, healing and happiness. I sent an email, arranged a meeting for upon my return to Australia and parked the idea right there.

Our next stop was **Salzburg** – what a magical city. If I'd ever move back to Austria, I'd live there for sure. I was truly looking forward to spending a few days with one of my closest friends from Vienna, Christian and his family, before we would all join forces with my best & longest standing friend Mona and her family as well as another family, close friends with Mona.

I felt so nurtured and cared for, cradled in between my two best friends, holding space for me as we said goodbye to the last year with Rob in it and welcome a new year full of hope and new beginnings.

We spent days building a snow dragon, with a head bigger than our kids and teeth we could hardly lift up – and yet there was some lightness in it all that our hearts needed. There was the real life magic that we were enchanted with during the 3D movie at Christmas. Now we were rolling in snow – literally.

The kids wiggled their way through an igloo that was the dragon's body; their cheeks red from the cold and excitement. All the adults helping out... We all need more play, more fun and more lightness in life. I'd love for you to stop for a moment, put this book down and make a little list of things you can do to allow more FUN into your life... Go on, I mean it!

Hold on, are you just reading on??

This list is *important*, trust me! It's part of your re-invention. You *create* the new you, starting *now*.

List of FUN things to do:

Ok... where were we? Oh, yes, the snow! Salzburg and its most beautiful countryside.
This was actually the second time we spent a very white Christmas and New Years in Austria when people told me that there won't be any snow. Well, just proves that I've got great connections up there! For a day or two we thought we wouldn't be able to leave, as we got a good half metre of snow over night; it was incredible.

Saying goodbye to Mona was tough for me. None of my friends know me as well as she does. We met in high school when we were 12 and 13. That's a lot of history we made together. Endless hours of "Wham" danced, listened & sung to, many meetings at the principal's office together (we won't go into detail), lots of laughter and also tears shared over the years. Mona also became my maid of honour; she flew all the way across the globe to witness our special day - and I had the same honour to be there for her special bond 3 years later. The deepest touching moment for me was when Mona came for my first birthday without Rob, a week that I will treasure forever. I remember feeling almost normal again for that *one week*, like nothing ever happened - only she could make me feel like that. I learned later that she had cancelled a family holiday in Tuscany to be able to be there for me; I was lost for words. Had I known that, I wouldn't have allowed it - hence she didn't tell me.

There was another person that was part of our circle... Anja. This is where we spent our next week, in **Gastein**, an amazing winter tourism destination south of Salzburg. I used to live there with my family from age 12 to almost 18. The place where I went to high school and sat through my HSC, just before moving to Vienna. It always gives me a warm fuzzy feeling going back to a place that seems to stand still in time. Just the other day I came to share my fondest memory from my very first night in Badgastein. It was before we moved there and my parents and I spent one night in an empty hotel called "Kaiserhof" that was supposed to be restored and reopened. My dad, a civil engineer, was asked to manage the project.

So, there I was, at the tender age of 12, an entire room to myself. The doors were so high and the atmosphere in the hotel spooky, I was certain it was full of ghosts. That night the snow was falling so thick from the sky - I opened the heavy doors to my very own balcony and stood there in the cold in my nightgown, feeling like a princess in an old castle. My mind was running wild with excitement, soft light from the promenade exposing some of the town in its darkness. It was remarkably quiet; as if we were the only 3 people in the entire town.

I took the boyzz back to that hotel and a flood of memories poured over me when ringing the doorbell. Trying to think of a good reason to request entry, we were simply buzzed inside.

I snapped a few photos, reminisced in my memories and just recharged my heart with gratitude for sharing this moment with my sons...

Jed turned 9 in Gastein.
We spent the day in a spa resort with thermal springs, water slides, and in- and outdoor pools. It was incredible, swimming in warm water and having thick snow fall onto our heads... but most magical of it all was watching their faces throughout the experience.

Flyn and Jed kept rolling outside in snow and then jumping back into the pool, steaming, at ease, frolicking... my heart was content.

Two days later we were all packed up for a very early drive to Salzburg airport. Anja and her husband drove us in one of the wildest snow storms I have ever experienced. I sat in the back between my boyzz, both leaning on me, falling asleep while my restless heart had me staring at the road ahead, as if I could avoid any danger and keep them safe.

I was contemplating sharing this little side story, yet I will, as it not only highlights a beautiful gift my sons both have, but also adds a little lightness and humour; so here it goes:

We had the strangest experience at Salzburg airport. We got there a little earlier than expected, chose to have breakfast after another emotional goodbye - and Jed noticed a man with a baby walk downstairs to the bathrooms. A minute later he came upstairs without the baby. When he told me, my heart sunk. I instantly had a really "wrong feeling" in my stomach, so I told them to stay where they were and I walked downstairs to the bathrooms.

Right in front of me was a baby change room and I noticed my hands started shaking. What on Earth was I thinking, walking downstairs by myself, leaving my boyzz unattended in an airport café? Carefully I opened the door and saw two pairs of men's legs behind a separator wall, one of them wearing red sneakers. I instantly closed the door again and ran upstairs. My heart was pounding; something definitely felt off. Not knowing who to contact, I told the lady at the café and she suggested that I notify the police. Since she was working on her own, she couldn't leave the place.

Again, I told Flyn and Jed to stay together and walked to the police station close by. On my left a guy sat with a large bag on the floor; he was wearing red sneakers! My heartrate went up again... I felt like I was in the middle of a crime investigation. At the police station nobody answered the locked door. I rang a few times... nothing. I walked back to Flyn and Jed. I felt so restless, worried about the little baby.

Eventually we packed up and I tried to ring the doorbell at the police one more time. The guy was still sitting there with his red sneakers, the same I had seen in the baby change room. It was unsettling to say the least. Again, no answer at the police station, so I decided to ask at the only counter that was open that early: a car rental place just opposite from the station. I briefly described what happened and the friendly ladies decided to contact the police. I left my details, it was all I could do, as we needed to proceed to our gate for boarding. On our way I watched two policemen walk in and downstairs to the bathrooms.

I felt a bit more at ease with police investigating. Nevertheless, I wanted to know that the baby was safe.

On board I was running the scene over and over in my head, wondering what else I could have done. When we finally took off, I noticed a lady sitting on the other side of the aisle, only one row ahead of me, feeding her baby. I was convinced it was the same baby we had seen "disappear" with the gentleman, who only half an hour earlier reappeared from the bathrooms at the airport without the baby. I didn't want to scare the mum and I also wanted to give her space while breastfeeding. Yet everything the baby was wearing and its size felt like it was the one that we thought had disappeared.

At long last when she finished feeding her baby, I approached the woman and carefully told her what we had witnessed at the airport. She almost burst into laughter and said how excited they were when their daughter had become the subject of a police investigation at her tender age only 4 months old, minutes before take-off. She had gone to the bathroom while the baby's dad collected their bags from the car to bring her downstairs to get changed before the flight. Due to us alerting police, they came and searched the airport for them, questioning the pair - only to find that everything was legit.

I was incredibly relieved to hear the entire truth about something that looked very suspicious to us. We were both truly delighted about the outcome - and yet I was also relieved to hear that we were both on the same page: better safe than sorry! I knew we had done the right thing...

About an hour later we landed in **Paris**. It was one of Flyn's wishes to eat escargots in Paris. I had found a lovely AirBnB in the middle of the French metropole, with a rather large window exposing the beautiful & impressive Tour d'Eiffel.
My friend Isa joined us for a couple of days and shared the excitement of going up on the world's most famous tower.

Isa and I met in advertising college in 1991-1993. My dad passed halfway through and Isa played a very important role in my life, keeping me on track. It was great to get to spend some quality time with her.

Each night we just sat and watched the lights in amazement. It was surreal, having the Eiffel tower right outside our window, flashing in its beautiful shape - I felt like in a movie scene. The tower was only 1.6km from our apartment. We walked there every day, did a touristy boat-ride to watch some of the main attractions - and then finally ordered escargot on our last day in Paris.

The scene was hilarious. The waiter was French as can be, with all its stereotypical behaviour traits when he served half a dozen of these little creatures in garlic sauce.

I made the biggest effort not to look disgusted and encourage Flyn in his endeavour. Until he offered me to try it, which of course I denied – and then he used the dad-card on me:
"Dad would've tried it with me!"
My eyes almost popped out of my head, as I listened to myself say "Ok!"

Hands down a mind-over-matter scenario!
Flyn tried them first, was quite proud of himself and said "hmm, not too bad...".

"Really?" I wondered whether he was trying to convince me or himself. Then it was my turn;
I cut the tiniest bit and courageously slipped it into my mouth, focusing hard not to set off my gag reflex. I am not even exaggerating; it was a true effort.
To my amazement even Jed came to the party and had a taste. It surely was a bonding moment for us. Shortly after we left 18 Euros, a not very excited waiter and 5 and a half escargots behind.

Next, we caught the TGV, France's high-speed train, to take us back to some childhood memories of mine in **Germany**. It was a nice way of experiencing the country and traveling in a different style.

Despite being a bit "out of our way" when it came to my travel plans, I had some "unfinished business" in Germany. I had completely lost touch with my god-daughter Maike, whom I just recently reconnected with – and in one of our many chats over the phone, she shared that I had promised her to take her out for ice cream next time I'd see her.

And so I did. We had two days of reconnecting, lots of laughter – my kids instantly liked her – and finally we had that big cup of ice cream, in the middle of winter!

Our final stop of the trip was my second-best kept secret, Flyn's birthday surprise. Three days of well needed fun, play and lightness for just the three of us, with the major highlight being a visit to Universal Studios at **Sentosa Island**.

It touched my heart, watching Alex the Lion dance with his furry friends, braving my fear for various rides and witnessing Jed losing a tooth in one of the lines. A perfect final stop before returning home to our life without Rob.

Love is all there is

The boyzz went back to school within a week of us arriving back home. It still felt surreal. Back to *normal*, a *new* normal, yet everything was *different...* *We* were different!

7.5 months after Rob's passing, I found myself on the floor of our living room, all by myself.
I noticed my emotions and thoughts creeping in. I literally pictured it as a dark hole opening up to my right. I recognised it as something that people would probably refer to as *depression*, something that I wasn't very familiar with - yet this felt like I would picture it.

I remember thinking "if I lean over to look down that hole, I might slip and it could swallow me whole". So I instinctively checked to my left and found an imaginary pile of happiness, a hill of hope and beautiful memories we had created since Rob's passing.

One thing became very clear to me. I knew exactly that I did not want to slide down that hole to my right. I was too scared that I wouldn't find my way back - yet at the same time I felt I didn't have it in me to climb that hill to my left. After the past 7.5 months of having every step of the way planned, I found myself with *nothing left*.
Nothing left to do, no plan ahead, no strength left. I felt empty.

So, I did what I could at that very moment: I allowed myself to sit in the middle and simply *observe*. I allowed myself to do nothing but that.

I observed my thoughts, my emotions, my memories, my state in this very moment. It was like putting myself into slow motion - and I had nowhere else to be. I realised that this was my very first moment since Rob's passing that I was not only by myself but also without any plans in place for the day ahead.

Ever since that phone call from the sergeant, telling me about my husband having "deceased in a hotel room in Perth" I had planned every step of the way. It was what kept me sane, gave me the feeling of being in control and enabled me to create happy memories for the boyzz.

And now I sat in absolute silence, experiencing how easy it could be to drift into nothingness, depression, darkness - yet I knew it was not where I wanted to be.
So, I became the observer. Allowed myself to feel that sense of emptiness. Not even in a negative way, more in a sense of space, vastness almost.

With that I continued to just *be*; with no agenda, no strength needed. Realising how easy it would've been to slide down that hole, not knowing how or if I could ever make it back - I also realised the choice I had to stay put and not move a muscle. Knowing in my heart that I had nothing left in this very moment - equally understanding what power this decision held: to do nothing but observe.

I fell in Love with "doing nothing". I spent 10 days just observing; not even being consciously aware of what I was doing at the time. It simply felt like *being on pause*.
In those 10 days I was reminded of the choice we had: we can live our lives from a place of fear or Love. And if we choose fear - no matter it be out of lack of strength, lack of awareness of our choice or being overwhelmed by reality, it is simply the feeling of being disconnected from Love.

The question is whether you are connected to it or not. Always. Because at the end of the day: **Love is all there is!**
Everything else is the absence of Love.

The further I walked my path, the more I realised that Love is like an eternal power source that I can plug into at any given moment. Yet it takes awareness, practice and dedication.

The day came to catch up with my new mentor, Mark Bowness. I knew I would work with him, even before we had our first meeting. A week later I sat in my first workshop recording my welcome video for my movement; and only another 2 weeks later I opened the doors to "Loving Life after Loss™" on 19th March 2019.

It felt like jumping off the cliff and growing my wings on the way down - only to realise that I already had them. Intuition allowed me to remember my wings; and bit by bit I learned how to use them, how to trust them (metaphorically speaking of course).

I felt I was always looked after. And it felt like I had a new found filter that I put on everything I heard, read, saw, felt, experienced... I had *created* that filter.

Mind you, there was plenty of doubt along the way - yet I seem to always find the right people, teachers, mentors, clients to believe in me, encourage further growth and hold space for me along the way.

I shared from my heart. And already in my first year I had plenty of opportunity to tell our story in podcasts and various media outlets. The biggest wave to date was caused by an **article in Mamamia**.

We featured in Apple's no.1 trending news story that day (even leaving news about the US president behind on no.3).

In one of the interviews, I remember the host summarising "So, instead of retreating to lick your wounds, like most people would, you went into *expansion*!"

I was equally touched and blown away by her statement. It was such a gift for me to see myself from her outside perspective; and I realised how right she was.

A few months later, sitting at the incredible Bald Hill overlooking the breathtaking start of the Illawarra region in NSW, Australia, I shared this beautiful gift with a close friend.

His response formed an extension of this gift: "So by going into expansion, you created a vacuum for even more Love to come in?!" Ha! I can hardly describe the joy I felt in my heart, hearing another outside perspective – allowing me to see myself in that light…

Now with all that in mind… going back to the introduction of my *first* book - can you see the similarities in the gifts I am continuously receiving? Here's a screenshot of it – wow!

> ## Introduction:
>
> I had this epiphany in front of our fire place, one night, sitting there wondering why I am handling Grief so differently to most people who I know. The answer was like a gift to me. I realised how much Love and support we are surrounded with – and all of a sudden I understood the concept of *abundance*, in my most vulnerable time in life.
>
> The concept of abundance is when *giving* and *receiving* are not only balancing, they are *dancing* with each other, creating a spiralling effect that draws more and more into its whirlwind of happiness and contentment; this is not created from wanting *more* in life, it is created from wanting to *give* more in life. What you get is an everlasting spiral that leaves your cup overflowing on a continuous basis, effortlessly.

Btw, have you ever noticed the word "dance" in abundance? Rob pointed that out to me, as he thought I'd love it – and of course I do! What a gift!

Intuition is your Guide

I had always been blessed with great intuition; it went through the roof when Rob passed. It was almost like all my senses strengthened – as if they all poured into me in his passing over.

Decision making was something that could easily send me into overthinking. In the weeks and months after Rob had died, I felt my intuition increase and eventually take over. I learned to trust it, lean into it. Whenever I tested or questioned it, I got very clear signs to step back into trusting. And so I did.

I also noticed that whatever I put out there, I received back. This is nothing new, it's universal law. Yet I noticed it in a truly amplified way. Like the moment in Vienna, when I knew I had something the world needed and then my mentor showed up. Just like in the beautiful saying "When the student is ready, the teacher appears!"

One of my biggest lessons in building and leading this movement was learning how to step back into *flow*. My supervision coach, an incredibly intuitive lady, told me just the other day "It's unnatural to always be in the flow. It's about learning how to reconnect with it when you need it!" That was a game changer for me. I had tried too hard to "keep the momentum up, always be in the flow, in my zone of genius" and did the exact opposite - I started pushing myself, but not in a healthy way.

Life is all about balance. Whatever is out of balance becomes unhealthy.
Letting go is not the same thing as letting yourself go.
Motivating yourself is so much healthier than pushing yourself.
Motivation is about connecting to who you want to be and showing up as that person, making decisions from that state of mind; trusting your intuition.

I'd like to share an incredible moment of intuition literally taking over. Somebody shared a very moving and intense piece by Alisha Bozarth about "Widowhood" in my group "Loving Life after Loss". I encourage you to look up her original piece, so you understand where I'm coming from with my different perspective.

I sat with it for a while. I noticed when reading it, how many filters my brain automatically switched on. How everything within me wanted to *shift* perspectives, suggest moving into *healing* rather than hurt...

So, with a whole lot of respect for the author and the biggest filter of *Loving Life after Loss* put on this very piece, I dared to share *my* version of her writing. I remember my heart was pounding, my hands were shaking - I feared judgement. I wasn't sure whether my group would be ready for what I had created. Yet my intuition just galloped into the sunset with me… and there I was. I took a deep and calming breath in and shared it.

At first, I only shared it in my group. Within minutes the first comments came in – all of them so welcoming and full of gratitude. It was another moment of realising that I had something my audience needed. Another moment of learning to trust my intuition. People needed to see and feel that they were not alone with what they felt deep inside and had never put words to – and now I had, I gave them those words; but even more so, I gave them tools and permission to re-invent themselves.

Within the next hour I busied myself sharing this very piece on as many platforms I could reach - my heart was overflowing with Love and purpose - I wanted the whole world to receive healing - and in this very moment I could see my own purpose in big bold letters:

I want to heal the world from grief!

Without further ado, I invite you to drop any potential judgement, open your heart and mind and read *my* version of Alisha Bozarth's piece about "Widowhood":

Widowhood is Re-Invention
(re-written & titled by Marie Alessi)

"Widowhood is more than just pain and losing your spouse. It is an opportunity for an alternate life. It is growing through adversity. Widowhood is going to bed and learning to embrace the stillness around you (sometimes even enjoying that bit of extra space that used to represent emptiness in those first intense times). Getting to know yourself within that solitude.

The night brings silence and a space to listen within, when all the drowning noise around you stops.

Widowhood is walking around the same house you have lived in for years and recreating spaces, colours and maybe even adjusting furniture to make it your home, suitable to your new situation. Because the home you had so far was created by a combination of you & him. And then they're not there. Now it's time to look within, allow yourself and dare to choose something different and new - maybe even something he wouldn't have chosen!

Widowhood is looking at all your dreams and plans you shared as a couple from your new & current perspective - it's a chance to check in with yourself "do I still want this?" "Would I still want to do this on my own?".

Finding excitement in the process of searching for new dreams that include simply you, are endless opportunities. And every small victory of creating new dreams for yourself beholds a hidden gift in adversity - something you might have not ever looked at before.

Widowhood is rediscovering everything you thought you knew about yourself. Your life had moulded together with another's and without them, you are invited to relearn all your likes, hobbies, *fears, goals. The renaissance of that new person may scare you, but makes you proud simultaneously.*

Widowhood is being a stranger in your own life. The unnerving feeling of watching yourself from outside your body, going through the motions of what was your life, but being detached from all of it. You don't recognise yourself. Your previous life feels but a vapor now gone, like a mist of a dream; you begin to wonder if it happened at all.

Widowhood is the irony of knowing if that one person was here to be your support, you also have the strength to grieve that one person. It is an honour to carry forward his memories while learning to trust your inner guidance, listen to your inner voice… You now have the challenging and empowering task of moving forward on your own.

Widowhood is despite missing the one person who could truly understand what is in your heart to share, to still share memories of his funny joke, the embarrassing incident, the fear compelling you or the frustration tempting you. To anyone else, you would have to explain why you choose to see this as an opportunity rather than defeat… and that is too much effort, so you keep it to yourself. Yet the empowerment grows within you.

Widowhood is the opportunity to re-identify yourself. *Who are you when not their spouse? What else do you want to do other than the things you planned together? What brand do you want to buy other than the one you two shared for all those years? What is your purpose now that the energy you invested into your marriage is yours to spend on anything you choose? Who is my closest companion now, when my other half isn't here?*

Widowhood is feeling restless because you & your home now feel different - just like your identity and the meaning you had attached to your partner, lover, friend, playmate, travel companion, co-parent, security and life. And you are navigating to an unknown destination.

Widowhood is living in a constant state of reinvention. With no hand to hold, nobody next to you by default and no partner to share your life with, it is your choice to learn to walk again, confidently on your own. Choose wisely whose company you invite into your life.

Widowhood can be being alone in a crowd of people. Yet it doesn't have to mean that you feel lonely - and it can even mean that you're happy. Allowing yourself to feel alive. It is looking back and moving forward. It is being hungry and tasting new things. It is preparing differently for every special event and maybe even celebrating more, as we know how precious life is.

Yes. It is much more than what society makes it to be. It is becoming a new person, in a way that you choose to be. It is embracing every emotion mankind can feel at the very same moment and allowing yourself to function differently in life to what anyone expects.

Widowhood is delicate. Widowhood is strength. Widowhood is fertile. Widowhood is rebirth.

Widowhood is life-changing and brings choices that are only yours to make."

Nurturing Healing Habits

There are certain habits we can create along our healing journey that are truly nurturing. One of them is allowing a different perspective on your current situation. To choose a simple and very generic example that most of you will be able to relate to, take this sentence:
"I had to move forward for my children!" "I forced myself to get out of bed every day, for them!" "I had no choice!"

Now, let's adjust this in wording, ever so slightly - and feel how everything changes instantly:
"I chose to move forward for my children!" "I chose to get out of bed every day, for us!" "I had a choice to make!"

See what I did there? One of the first things when I hear a mum say these words "I had to..." is making them aware that they *didn't have* to. They *chose* to. Unfortunately there are plenty of examples out there where different choices were made. Drugs, alcohol and sadly often suicide. If you're reading this, you did *not* choose any of these, you chose to *live*.
Congratulations, no matter how challenging it was for you, you chose to live! It is time for you to own your choices. This is called empowerment. And this might be your very moment of stepping into it. Welcome to my world.

This is exactly what I want for you. "Happy Healing" is brought to you with the intention to open your heart to healing - so I'd love to share some very hands-on tools with you that you can use immediately.

Let me get right into it, starting with one of my favourite exercises I have shared numerous times over the years. It is an exercise for when you feel there's no way out, or in no way could you ever open your heart to healing. I am not attempting to take that away from you, yet here's something you can try; I call it "The Colour Orange".

I invite you to actively participate now - consider it as planting a seed for your healing tree. Today I'd like you to make a list of as many things you can find in the colour orange (or replace it with whatever *your* favourite colour is). I challenge you to find at least 20 things and collect them on a list you actually write down.

You will soon find how easy it is to do so. The more you look, the more things you will find. Even just looking around my desk where I am writing this book right now, I can see an orange metal clip, an orange folder, an orange ring binder, an orange highlighter, an orange pencil; the picture behind me is a beautiful painting of the Opera House in Sydney, with the predominant colour being – you guessed it – orange!

So, this took me less than a minute and I already found 6 things. Looking outside through my glass door, I can see a metal bucket, a plastic shovel, the reflector on my son's bike, a faded frisbee, a window cleaning tool - all in the colour orange.
So, round it up to 2 minutes and 11 things. I bet your list will be a lot longer than just 20 items, but I want to make this easy for you.

Now, when you play this game for an entire day, you will see how hard it is to stop the next day. You will find so many things, all in the colour orange! Why? Because this is what you put your focus on. It's like being in the market for a particular car and suddenly you will see that same model everywhere.

On day 2 I'd like you to replace the colour orange with the *emotion* you miss the most. For the sake of keeping it easy and also quite generic, I choose Love. Ok, it's also my favourite - obviously - and for a lot of you this will be the first thing you miss when your loved one passes. I invite you to find as many "images of Love" out there as you can.

Love comes in many forms. It can be a mum carrying her baby, a couple walking hand in hand, a movie that you watch, even a lady at the counter of your supermarket giving you a genuine smile or hello. For others that might be sunshine or a gorgeous tree, a flower growing out of concrete at the side of the road… The possibilities are endless. Play it for an entire day and see how many "scenarios of Love" you can find.

"The colour Orange" isn't designed to *replace* anything or anyone, it is designed to experience first-hand how you can choose your focus. How you can retrain your brain to find beauty in everything you look at, everywhere you go. By doing so you will fill that emptiness with warmth and beauty. And whatever you focus on, grows.

And as always, the more you put in, the more you get out. Give it your all. See how well you can do in one day, in 2 days… This is stepping back into empowerment. You can do this!

All these little discoveries I made along the way became an integral part of my first healing journey I created for clients - let me share the outline of it with you. I have called this journey "From Grief to Relief". And for those who have never even toyed with the idea of allowing healing in, this can be your very first encounter and I am truly excited for you!

Allow me to introduce it step by step:

1. **Separate who you have lost from what you have lost!**
   It is an important exercise to separate these two - and I will share with you how.

   One of the things that came up for me when Rob passed was "feeling safe". I don't like being alone in the dark - never have. With Rob I felt safe, protected.
   Or the perfect hug. My Love languages are "physical touch" and "quality time".
   If you're not familiar with Dr. Gary Chapman's work, I urge you to check it out!
   So, when Rob died, I truly missed feeling protected, missed his hugs and simply feeling him close to me…

2. **How can I create what I miss?**
   Nothing and nobody can ever replace what Rob and I had. And I want to emphasise again that this exercise is *not* about *replacing* anyone. Yet it is about *creating* what you miss for yourself - taking charge and here I say it one more time: stepping back into empowerment.

   One of the first things I did was pushing my bed into the corner; it made me feel more "cradled in" and *safe*. I also made sure that I checked whether the front and back door were locked before I went to bed (despite living in a very safe neighbourhood).

   And hugs… Family Therapist Virginia Satir says "We need 4 hugs a day for survival, 8 hugs a day for maintenance and 12 hugs a day for growth." Boy, have I got some catching up to do… I am lucky that my sons love hugging me (still!) and my friends all know me as a hugger. It's not the same like hugging my husband of course – yet we still need hugs!

3. **The Hole & the Hill experience**
   This is the exact experience I described at the beginning of the chapter "Love is all there is". To summarise: I found myself sitting between something that felt like a hole to my right, that I could've easily slipped into; something that felt like depression. And to my left I felt this little pile of happiness, new memories we had created since Rob's passing, yet I felt I had no strength left to climb it for a better view. So I sat in the middle and allowed myself to do nothing but *observe*!

   What I want you to take away from this is: when things get overwhelming, *allow* yourself to simply observe. Nothing else. No pressure. No judgement. Simply notice your emotions and the choices you *do* have!

4. **Thought Patterns & Language**
   When you observe, you will also notice what kind of language you use - when communicating with others - and even more so important: the words you use when talking to yourself.
   Be your own best friend. Become your biggest supporter. Treat yourself with kindness and Love.

   What would you say to yourself if you were talking to your best friend? You'd be so supportive and encouraging! Step into *that* perspective – you've got this, trust me!

5. **Guilt, Secondary Gain & Forgiveness**
   One thing I hear over and over in my work with beautiful souls is that they feel *guilty* when experiencing joy. As if betraying their loved one. Here's the thing: society has done a pretty good job in convincing us that the amount of grief we feel and portray equals the amount of Love we felt for that person…

   I don't want to deny that the deeper you love someone the more it can hurt when they go before you. However, I have also learned that we can turn that same Love into joy – in the way we honour our loved ones. Please allow that to sink in for a moment. I remember times when Rob and I had this talk "if something was to happen to you…" and it always ended in both of us saying "I would want you to create the happiest life possible for you and the boyzz!" See, that's what Love is. Love would never suggest you cry for the rest of your life. Love means you want the other person to be *happy*, no matter what.
   This is big. It is truth. Love is just that simple.

   And this brings me to the next point: as hard as it is to accept, when you hold on to hurt despite what we just covered, there is *secondary gain* involved. A term often used by coaches, meaning: there's something you get out of *staying in that pain*, otherwise you wouldn't do it.

Nobody chooses consciously to stay in pain, it mostly happens on a subconscious level. And sometimes it is as simple as us having been taught all our lives "If you love someone and (s)he dies, you need to mourn as long as you can, maybe even for the rest of your life, to prove how much you loved her/him." What would our loved ones say to that? Would they agree? Certainly not!

I also talk about *forgiveness*, as it often comes hand in hand with guilt. Forgiveness is an integral part of healing. I once read this statement: "Not forgiving is like drinking poison and expecting the other person to die." Pretty brutal, don't you think? Yet not forgiving truly is like poisoning yourself, hence I always suggest you don't leave yourself off that list when it comes to people you want to forgive.

Check out my *forgiveness meditation* as one of my "free gifts" at the end of this book.

6. **Hidden Gifts & Re-Identification**
Here is something I have learned throughout adversity: it *always* comes with hidden gifts. Sometimes they stay hidden - yet once we open our hearts and start discovering them, they just keep coming. I have been blessed with many gifts - my biggest one was recognising the soul contract I had with Rob. Once I had this realisation I opened my heart more and more to what that actually meant - and how much *Love* was involved in our contract. I see it as the gift that keeps on giving and now creates ripples around the world - just as it does for you now, by reading my book, our story...
My heart is at peace!

And for me to allow those hidden gifts in, I took myself through a process of re-identification. Look at all the roles you play in your life right now, all the labels you wear:

wife, mother, friend, colleague, leader, soccer coach, taxi driver – whatever these might be in your life.
How have they changed after your loved one's passing? Which of them have changed? Which new labels have you received? And do you like them? I certainly do not like the label of a widow. I only just looked up the origin of the word and almost fell off my chair: Old English *widewe*, from an Indo-European root meaning 'be empty'; compare with Sanskrit *vidh* 'be destitute'. Really?
Well, this brings me back to my version "Widowhood is Re-Invention" (in chapter Intuition). You can *create* who you want to be.

7. **Role Reversal – the Letter**
The following exercise not only takes time, but I highly recommend you take all the above steps in preparation for your own healing journey. Open your heart and trust the process. I suggest for you to do so *before* you actually continue reading or doing this exercise.
I also suggest you do this with enough time and space around you - no disruptions.

Take a moment to truly connect with your loved one, close your eyes, breathe it in. Then I want you to look at *yourself* from *their* perspective, through *their* eyes.
And from *that* perspective I want you to write a letter - from your loved one to you.

Mine started like this: "Dear Marie, I am so incredibly proud watching you with the boyzz. I see the life you are creating for them, just like we talked about..."
This will not only give you an outside perspective, even more so – it will give you a very accurate perspective from somebody who loves and knows you so well.

Remember: *Love is all there is*. Sit in *Love* when working through this healing journey. Love is an eternal power source that you can plug into at any given stage. The more you do it, the easier it becomes!

For those of you who want more detail on "From Grief to Relief" you can find the entire healing journey with videos in my movement "Loving Life after Loss™".

All details can be found on **MarieAlessi.com**.

Gratitude is your SuperPower

When Rob passed, I was half way through a book called "The Magic" by Rhonda Byrne.

It is not a book that you would just read in one go; rather a workbook, with 30 short chapters on how to *practise* gratitude. I loved the little exercises, they really shifted things for me, brought awareness into areas that were lacking it.

With Rob's passing I stopped with the book and its exercises.

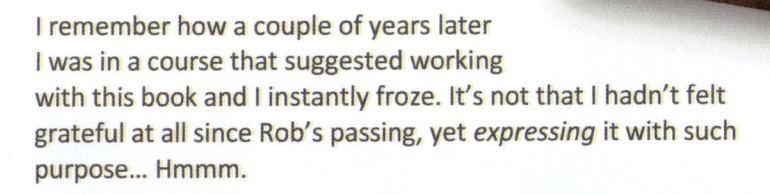

I remember how a couple of years later I was in a course that suggested working with this book and I instantly froze. It's not that I hadn't felt grateful at all since Rob's passing, yet *expressing* it with such purpose... Hmmm.

I sat with it for a couple of days and then decided. I knew it was time for me to pick that book back up. And I also knew it was more than just that. There was healing in that process. There is healing in gratitude.

It comes back to simplifying when you are in overwhelm. We tend to overcomplicate our life when we are overwhelmed. Gratitude reminds us of what we *have* and what we *can* do, in a time where we feel we have lost so much. So, expressing gratitude takes all of that a step further. It highlights it, amplifies it - and it allows Love back into your heart.

I like simplicity. Simple steps I can follow. "The Magic" sure does offer simple steps. One by one it addresses every area of your life and allows you to shed the light of gratitude onto it. Gratitude became my SuperPower.

Needless to say, I have finished the book by now – even though it is never meant to be finished, rather to be started and continued. It is designed to install this as a new habit in your life, something that comes so natural to us.

The magic that happens for me when practising gratitude is that it brings me back into the now, the presence, the current moment. What is the one thing or that one person you are grateful for right now? In this very moment, reading my book. Something or somebody you do have in your life right now...

And even if your mind might still be drifting back to that one person who has died in your life, then I encourage you to find that one thing you are so grateful for that you have learned or received from this person - this also brings you back into the now.

When a person dies, not all gets lost or dies with that person.

My heart is literally overflowing with gratitude for all the gifts Rob has brought into my life.
- ♥ The Love I was blessed to experience
- ♥ The home we have created together
- ♥ Our two boyzz that bring so much Joy into my life
- ♥ Seeing Rob live on in both of them
- ♥ The concept of choices that helps me every day
- ♥ My intuition and strength I have been blessed with
- ♥ The global movement I have founded, based on all these gifts
- ♥ Being able to share my message and heal so many people
- ♥ Changing the stigma of grief

Just to name a few... We all have those gifts – yours are most likely different to mine. Yet you do have them – and I am happy to help you discover them.

I'd like to finish this book with 3 amazing stories and testimonials that I am also incredibly grateful for to share with you. I am honoured that these women have given me their permission to share their very personal words and what effect it had once they allowed me to walk part of their path with them. I am honoured by the trust they have put in me and deeply touched by the transformation in their lives.

I want you to understand that *they* did all the work, I was just in the right place at the right time to hold space for them and hand them the tools.

Without further ado, please meet Shelyna, Terri and Paulina
#standingovations

Shelyna Stefansson

"Life changes on a dime. We can never really know from one moment to the next how it will unfold. For me, my life took a huge turn at the start of Canadian Thanksgiving in 2019. My mother-in-law passed away and the long weekend resulted in me holding my husband close all the while attending to arrangements for us to travel across the country to be with his family.

It was a hard and sad holiday and I felt useless to my husband's grief. Little did I realize that this would be just the start of an even tougher journey for me. On the Tuesday following, my husband's heart gave in to his pain and he died in my arms of a massive heart attack. Instead of us travelling to be with his family, each of them dropped everything and instead came to my side.

The youngest of five children, he was the baby and far too young to have left our world so soon. That day in the hospital has become one of my fondest memories of our time together, strange as that may sound. It was three hours of laughter, love, and hope before he succumbed to joining his mother. It's not easy to comprehend how or what happened to me that day. I think the best way to explain it is to tell you that I felt like every ounce of his love transferred into me and became my lifeline. I was consumed by love, then and since. I was enamored by the people that came pouring into my space to offer their support, by the gifts that accompanied them, and by the memories that I held within me. I felt no disbelief, anger, or denial; the feeling of love was too intense and carried me into each hour of my loss.

I had faced adversities before and one thing was certain, I was determined to pull myself through this and find happiness for myself again. I vowed to do the hard work in healing, whatever it took. A dear friend reached out to me only seven weeks after he died, with a recommendation to join Loving Life after Loss. She had stumbled upon it herself and felt that it may give me some peace to be surrounded by others that were experiencing loss as well. Was it the name of the group that called to me? Or was it Marie, with her authenticity and a big heart that was extended out to heal the world? Perhaps it was both. I was drawn in from the very start, and began each day, every day, by listening to her lives, reading the posts, and drinking in the hope of what her movement had to offer. I rarely got off the couch in those weeks and months following his passing and wasn't taking care of myself at all. I cried, I focused on that love that seemed bigger than anything else in the whole world, and I followed Marie's every word.

Joining her programs, one after the other, wasn't a choice for me. It was a necessity.
I needed what she was so generously offering. Over the course of the next six months, I began to find myself and learn more about me and who I am. I continued to embrace that extraordinary feeling of love that had enveloped me at the start, and I added personal awareness, growth, and knowledge. In short, I was learning how to love me.

My future felt shaky and unknown. I no longer knew what I wanted to do with my life ahead; everything that I had once anticipated didn't make sense anymore. Yet here I was, falling in love with the person that was emerging from within me, and I felt full of hope, joy, and anticipation to keep discovering more about who I am. I fell in love with the sky, the forest, the waters. I was in love with birds chirping, flowers growing, and clouds passing overhead.

I started to walk daily. I was taking in everything nature had to offer, as though I had never really seen it before. It was then, in those glorious days of rediscovery, that I realized I would be okay. That I could be sad, miss him desperately, and still walk into a future that had no resemblance whatsoever to what I once expected. I didn't need to know what my tomorrows had in store for me. I just simply had to embrace today, and each day, with a yearning to keep learning and discovering what life has to offer.

If I could go back to the beginning when my husband died, and do it all again, I wouldn't change a thing. I would join the movement, and every program, and follow my heart to wherever it takes me. I am grateful that I chose to invest in me, and I finally understand these gifts that were bestowed on me by losing him. His death gifted me even more love."

♥ ♥ ♥

Terri, a Motherling

"Ryan is my only son. He slipped away when I wasn't looking. In the moment I knew exactly where he was, who was there to cradle him in loving arms.
Ryan and I exhaled in unison. We have always been and will always be one in our hearts.

Ryan has gifted me 3 light beings – 2 boys and a wee girl – my Glamkids. All have the Ryan factor; the look, the cheekiness, the determination to be right all the time – the biggest heart; they shine so lovingly and bright in my life – my slice of Ryan the Lion forever. Their brilliance blinds me.

Familiar as we all are here, that numbing journey of the first day, night, week, month, year, birthdays, Mother's Day, Christmas – for me it was a very sacred decision to bring Ryan home to the place he grew up.

Family and his closest mates gathered to share amazing stories about their lives together; soccer, surfing, boxing & lots of pubs and weekends, being larrikins. I am forever grateful that I listen to my inner pendulum; tears that grown young men could share in private, so beautiful, so honouring. We as a family anointed him, loved him. I know he was standing amongst us, saying "Get the beers on!"

We could all let his physical body go – in June his mates organised a paddle out at his favourite beach. This was my day of spiritual reckoning, where all was as it should be. It was the most incredible way to honour Ryan and his children. Both Ryan's young boys paddled out into the mighty sea with their Pa Pa. So courageous, so strong, so like their dad.

As 2019 came to a close, my 60th birthday loomed before me. I was there but not present; talking but not really speaking; I was 2 people in 2 different realms, spirit & Earth. My outward voice echoed up through the top of my head – divine human encounters began to cross my path – ocean swimming & breath work meditation with my coach Kim.

I learned to breathe again and be silent. And I even home-schooled a Magpie family of 4 for two seasons!

Then Marie Alessi randomly popped up in my newsfeed at 3 am; I was wide awake, unable to sleep. That was the moment that Marie & Loving Life after Loss entered my life.

To say I was extremely resistant to joining any "grief groups" is an understatement – but there was intrigue into the name of the group – and then I had a telephone call with Marie herself, a human voice, who was in the midst of her journey of the loss of her husband Rob.

This made her real. And this is how I began my journey with "Loving Life after Loss".

To conclude my story, let me share what I sent to Marie after working closely with her for more than a year:

„Marie that was a post full of energy & personal strength & how far you have come & encouraged us to come with you ❤️

I have noticed that my voice sounds different, it feels different as I speak, so I believe I'm finding my very own truth within this heart felt journey of the loss of my son Ryan.

I seek balance and integration of my mind, body & my soul – there has been so much numbness & physical trauma to my body, but I feel a shift and a greater willingness to listen and apply the lessons that are continuously coming my way; and that can be meeting random people or animals or things I thought I had lost suddenly turning up.

I truly want to encourage anyone here who is looking for the Loving of life after loss to engage in one of the many programs that Marie offers; they can be life changing in a positive and courageous way if you allow it to be – Mother's Day has come and passed, for the 2nd year; so yes, I did prepare, emotionally I calmed myself within and opened my heart to the family I was going to be sharing the day with.

I was nothing but loved and cared for – I was scared I would close myself off, feel sorry for myself; but when I stopped feeling frightened, I actually felt expanded.

I hope that this helps one person to take a little step forward in your life – painful yes at times but within this amazing group we find so much strength and support – sharing ourselves with each other.

In so many ways we are all here together for the right reason ❤️💕

Love, Me 🧜‍♀️💜❤️
From the Sea"

♥ ♥ ♥

Paulina Leech

"I have been lucky to live on this earth for 39 years so far, travelling in the company of my wonderful family – my husband James and our two girls, Nisa & Cora.

In 2020 we were blessed with a surprise pregnancy, our third child. We didn't find out the sex of the baby, we were all so very excited to meet the newest member of our family.

During the pregnancy we enjoyed bonding with them, and I especially grew a strong bond with our little one. On the first day of October, 2020, our baby stopped moving, but this wasn't confirmed until the next day, by ultrasound.

I had previously experienced deaths of members of my extended family and close friends, but nothing compared to the loss of someone from my immediate family, a child, it was my worst nightmare come true. Our little angel was born three days later on the 5th October, at 35 weeks gestation in the birth pool at the local hospital.

Our beautiful girl, Reyna, with a shock of dark hair and a peaceful look on her face, was born in the presence of her dad James, her sisters Nisa and Cora, and our two beautiful midwives, Sam and Bec. We were lucky to have beautiful photographs taken of our little angel, thanks to the organisation Heartfelt.

We were able to spend a whole day and night with Reyna, thanks to the use of the hospital's 'cold cot', before saying our final goodbye to her and going home. It was a difficult time, yet we as a family came together like never before. It was devastating to have lost our youngest daughter, yet we gained so much after her death – so much love, between us and from family and friends, as well as gratitude, empathy, wisdom and valuable lessons.

We were also lucky to have my mum come visit from NSW for two months, after quarantining for two weeks. She lost her first daughter, my older sister, at 40 weeks' gestation, so having her here with us was a wonderful gift, her empathy and presence was healing to us all.

Fast forward to early 2021 and we discovered I was pregnant with our 4th child. We were all over the moon, and despite feeling a bit apprehensive, we were still hopeful that things would be different this second time around. As the pregnancy progressed, we found out that things were not as well as they seemed with our little one, or myself.

I had complete placenta previa, which meant a caesarean birth would be the only option, also I was found to have severe polyhydramnios, excessive amniotic fluid. As time went on and my belly grew beyond normal proportions, our little one also grew, and with their growth a myriad of health issues were also revealed.

These issues were highly concerning, including hydrocephalus (excess fluid in the brain), and a diaphragmatic hernia, in which our baby's organs were pushing into a hole in their chest cavity, pushing one lung and the heart to one side, restricting their lung capacity and the heart function. I was in and out of hospital, and in the last month was in hospital for 2 weeks before our baby was born.

By that stage I had multiple ultrasounds, tests, was unable to walk very far and had endured the amnio-reduction procedure four times, in an attempt to reduce pressure on my placenta and on our baby.

While I was in hospital, I barely got to see James and our girls, we had never been away from each other for so long before and it was difficult, for all of us.

On the morning of Friday 13th August, one of the doctors came to my hospital room and suggested that the caesarean be done that day, as his colleagues had concerns that I may experience a placental abruption and lose the baby. So hasty plans were made for our daughters with some new yet wonderful friends, and James and I were suited up and taken into theatre.

After some time, our baby made their entrance into the world, then James announced to me it was a boy! We didn't get time to talk about it at that moment, but I knew his name was Dorian, the name we had always kept if we ever had a boy. The surprised, joyful smile stayed on my face for some time.

We were advised beforehand that our baby would need to be taken to the N.I.C.U, and that is what happened. When I came out of Recovery, my bed was wheeled to Recovery where I met up with James, and we both were taken to where our baby boy Dorian was. He was in a tiny cot, hooked up to lots of tubes and some machines, including a ventilator, which made his breath rattly and loud.

We were told that he had been given morphine, to keep him comfortable and free from any pain. His tiny body was carefully moved from his cot to my chest, where he lay for a long while, then he was gently moved to lie on James' naked chest.

At that point the head paediatrician came to speak to us to let us know that, after some tests, Dorian was found to also have thickening in part of his heart, which was making it beat sluggishly, and he was deteriorating quickly.

We made the heart-breaking decision to have his ventilator turned off. We were fortunate that our new friend who was babysitting our girls was able to bring them quickly to the hospital, where they were able to meet their new little brother, and say their last goodbyes to him. It was like he was waiting for them, as not long after, his heart stopped beating.
We were so fortunate to once again receive the gift of having a photographer from the organisation Heartfelt take photos of our littlest angel, dressed up in a tiny, colourful onesie, the only clothes he'd ever wear. His body was placed into a 'cold cot', and we were able to spend a whole day and night with him, and after saying our final goodbyes, I stayed in hospital for one more night before going home with James and our girls.

Having been through Reyna's passing, Dorian's was in some ways easier, knowing that he escaped a life of possibly many difficulties, pain and permanent disabilities, yet it was still devastating, knowing we'd missed the chance of having him here with us.

After Reyna's stillbirth, a friend mentioned this Facebook group to me, called "Loving Life after Loss", and she suggested that I join as I might find it helpful after our loss. So I did.
And while I wasn't an active participant, I enjoyed reading the posts, the poems and quotes that everyone shared.

It was sad yet incredibly validating, seeing so many different people going through grief and being brave enough to share their thoughts and feelings with others. I was in the deep end of my grief at that point, it was raw and tumultuous, I felt such deep love in my heart yet so much painful sadness, I felt like communicating with others was too hard for me, so I retreated and felt I needed time alone to heal.

Having been a passive participant in "Loving Life After Loss", I became active by sharing Dorian's birth story on there. Marie reached out to me and we really connected, she was warm, compassionate and so genuine, I also really admired her outlook on life.

Later in the year I completed one of Marie's "Blank Canvas" programs, along with a small group of fellow participants. Over the eight weeks we connected via Zoom calls and got to know each other, share our stories, feelings, laughter, tears, and much love through our screens.

It was a wonderful time of healing for me, feeling the comforting solidarity from the others every week as we navigated through challenges we were facing in our lives at the time, while also sharing the moments of beauty and our gratitude for those things.

I went from being directionless in my life to feeling like I had more purpose and more to live for, I was able to finally see outside of myself and see the possibilities before me that I hadn't been able to, or wanted to, see beforehand.

Completing the "Blank Canvas" program was a turning point for me. I felt like I had conquered some enormous challenges and I felt liberated in myself. I was able to breathe again and continue to live my life in a different way, by looking forward to the future with my family, and having done the work to free myself from living a life of grief, like I was expecting to happen.

My favourite quote is by Rumi, and says, "The cure for the pain is in the pain." In the last year, I have learnt to understand this quote in its entirety. Since the passing of our two beautiful babies, I have struggled through indescribable pain, yet I have also experienced such beautiful moments on this journey of grief as well.

For myself, I have found that experiencing such pain has broken me open to so many feelings and showing me new opportunities for healing in my everyday life. Some days I have all but blocked myself off from experiencing the emotions of grief, and I have suffered greatly in later days. Other times when I have surrendered myself to feeling whatever pain may come,
I have had breakthroughs in my healing, feeling like the love inside of me has grown exponentially afterwards.

This journey of grief looks so different for every person who walks it, my wish is that every person reading this book understands that, and will go easy on themselves as they navigate this new chapter of their lives. I wish you all much love, strength, and hope for your futures."

♥ ♥ ♥

Can you see why I am so deeply touched by the trust I am given every day?
Gratitude can make all the difference in your life, once you start putting it into practice.
I make a choice every single day, what perspective I want to live my life from.

**Healing is a choice.
Make it.**

Much Love x

Marie

About the Author

I realised shortly after my husband died that *everything* leading up to that moment was preparing me to not only *cope* with his death; it was the beginning of a journey that was even bigger than the two of us; a journey full of Love beyond the physical realm, one of hope and empowerment and inspiration. Rob has been my guide in this life and continues to be from the other side!

I was born in Austria in 1972. Growing up with 4 adopted siblings as the only one born into the family was challenging. Yet it gave me tools and skills that proved to be very handy one day; and an everlasting desire of seeking my most authentic self. I believe I have found it.

Something deep within my heart kept calling me to come to Australia many years ago; well before my first flight to Sydney in 1997. I finally felt home. My heart flourished, my perspectives changed, I knew I had to move here permanently – and so I did, in 2004.

I started the journey home to myself!

Only 10 months later I met Rob – and through him a Love I had never experienced before – genuine, unconditional Love from the purest soul I was blessed to marry.

We were gifted with two most precious and gorgeous boys, soon to be gentlemen.

My career took me from advertising to coaching, a journey into self-development, which has been rewarding on so many levels. After running my own coaching practice for 7 years, I stepped away and into my next chapter of being an Influencer, Speaker and Author.

I made it my mission to heal the world from grief.

Free Gifts

Thank you for reading my story, I feel truly blessed to be able to share it with you.

Allow me to give you some gifts as a little thank you for buying my book. I believe these gifts can help you a lot in dealing with the unthinkable, should you choose to accept them.

Upon entering my group, I offer a 3-part video series – I invite you to join us:

https://facebook.com/groups/LovingLifeAfterLoss

As a member of my group, you have access to the entire Healing Journey I touch on in my chapter "Nurturing Healing Habits", in a lot more detail and with video instructions. Simply head to the "guide" section in my group to find "**From Grief to Relief**".

And as promised, in that very journey you will also find my **Forgiveness Meditation** I wanted to share you.

For further information, upcoming programs & retreats or simply to get in touch, please visit:

MarieAlessi.com

♥ ♥ ♥

Thankyous

Would you believe me if I said this is the hardest part of writing my book? Not that I would find it hard *thanking* people, but I understand that there are *a lot more* people to thank for than I could possibly fit in one chapter... Yet there are a few that really stood out for me over the past couple of years, whom I'd really love to mention here:

Mona – first and foremost for flying around the globe once again, to spend an entire week with me for my birthday. This one week allowed me to feel *normal* again, me again, light.
This lightness was such a gift to me – I don't know where I would've been without you.

Des – for not only driving down from the Mountains to be with me the night before the funeral, but also sitting behind me during the funeral. Your strength held me; your presence was invaluable for me.

Jo – for sitting with me after coming home from Perth. You held space for me – and your empathy touched me so deeply.

Ricardo – every single conversation with you is priceless. You are an incredible gift in my life and I am eternally grateful for our connection.

Blair – you rocked my world... thank you for holding space for me throughout this enormous life lesson that became such an important part of my healing.

Romana – you kept me sane in the most intense part of my healing journey. You have become such an integral part of my inner circle in record time.

Steve – for picking up the pieces over and over, until I was finally whole again.

I want to thank you all for loving me through the storm!

♥ ♥ ♥

Printed in Great Britain
by Amazon